Prime Time Apparitions

Prime Time Apparitions

R. Zamora Linmark

Hanging Loose Press
Brooklyn, New York

Copyright © 2005 by R. Zamora Linmark

Published by Hanging Loose Press, 231 Wyckoff Street, Brooklyn, NY 11217-2208. All rights reserved. No part of this book may be reproduced without the publisher's written permission, except for brief quotations in reviews.

www.hangingloosepress.com

Printed in the United States of America
10 9 8 7 6 5 4 3 2 1

Hanging Loose Press thanks the Literature Program of New York State Council on the arts for a grant in support of the publication of this book.

Cover art: *Bigyan Mo Po Kami...* [Give Us This Day] by Marvin "Bin" Samonte
Cover design by Marie Carter

Library of Congress Cataloging-in-Publication Data

Linmark, R. Zamora.
   Prime time apparitions / R. Linmark Zamora.
     p.cm.
     ISBN 1-931236-46-1 (cloth) -- ISBN 1-931236-45-3 (pbk.)
    1. Phillipines--Poetry. I. Title.

PS3576.A475P75 2005
811'.54--dc22

2005040209

Produced at The Print Center, Inc. 225 Varick St., New York, NY 10014, a non-profit facility for literary and arts-related publications. (212) 206-8465

Acknowledgments continue at rear of book.

CONTENTS

Screening Desire

A Letter to Claire Danes from a Fan in Manila	15
Screening Desire	17
ESL, or English as a Sign Language	19
The Superstar Talks to Her Award-Winning Role, Flor Contemplacion	20
Manila, My Manila: Wish List for a Day	23
If I a Gay	24
Rhapsody	25
Tita Aida	28
Says the Kiwi Bird	31
This Poem Is Called "Waiting" or "The Problems of Using Metaphors in Confessional Poetry"	34
On Days That Break Us	36

Slippery When English

After Carl Dreyer's *Ordet* (*The Word*)	39
A Modest Manila Proposal	42
Slippery When English	45
And Yet	46
Why Cicadas Have More Fun	47
The Muse This Time	48
Moo	50
Caliban's Epilogue	53
First Lessons	54
Academia 101	55

Itinerary

Errata	59
A Portrait of the Poet, Smallkid Time	61
Auntie Mary	65
Sensory for Nine	67
Valentine's Day	72
A Letter To Urbana in America From Her Seventy-Year-Old Sister Felisa	74
Requiem	76
What Some Are Saying About the Body	77
Exodus	81
Itinerary	83

*For Pamel, Tyler, Precious, & Alexander:
four navigational points to home*

For my grandparents, Purificacion and Frank Linmark

&

*In memory of my grandfather,
Fernando Zamora (1919 to 2001)*

"Fluft drin Yalerick Dwuldum prastrad mirplush."
—Jonathan Swift, *Gulliver's Travels*
(Voyage to Laputa)

Zack: That's That

Parts of Zack's life climb in and out of his writings, but he takes great liberties with them, undressing himself of them to such an extent that he becomes, on his page, a character he has never met.

Perhaps it has something to do with having so many tongues in his mouth: two Filipino dialects, Hawaiian pidgin, and five languages, including his newly acquired Japanese.

Very difficult to be a fixed anything in the kind of locating of the self that language is supposed to be when there are several of them doing the locating.

So it's a good thing Zack is a trickster who is married to airplanes that land only temporarily in the maps he unsticks from his shoes, so he can delight the friends and admirers caught in them with his momentary and scintillating presence.

He knows how to laugh in all his languages and, fortunately for us, funnels his laughter onto the page in English, enjoys kicking the slats out from under. He is very well-read, borrows characters, landscapes, and conniption fits from writers he admires, as well as from writers who raise his hackles and whom he considers fair game for parody.

Zack is hyphenated but, unlike Richard Rodriguez, if you find his book in a hyphenated part of the bookstore, he does not ask that you re-shelve it in astrology. Although the hyphen is bothersome, Zack understands its "toolness." To him it's an irony bar, a teeter totter, a tightrope in the middle of which he very agilely balances on a whimsical chair.

Zack has many subjects and is fearless, as he has always been since the day I found him, an undergraduate at the University of Hawaii at Manoa, waiting for me outside the English department office. He had just returned from Barcelona, where he wasn't supposed to have been. Of the pages he showed me that day, only three lines wound up not in the wastebasket; but their honesty, humor, intelligence, courage, and imagination became the toolbox he has carried ever since.

Faye Kicknosway

Screening Desire

A Letter to Claire Danes from a Fan in Manila

> *"The place just fucking smelled of cockroaches. There's no sewage system in Manila, and people have nothing there. People with, like, no arms, no legs, no eyes, no teeth. We shot in a real psychiatric hospital...."*
> Claire Danes to *Premiere* magazine

Dear Claire—
It is ghastly indeed: this city
crowded with cockroaches and people
who walk without legs, drive long
chrome-plated coffins without arms,
and stare imperiously at you
without eyes. Not to mention
squatters sleeping on stilts,
island panhandlers, again without arms
and legs, highway beggars,
again without eyes and hair,
and sidewalk dwellers whose walls
are painted with huge signs
reminding people not to dump trash,
piss, shit. By the way,
how was San Francisco? Are you now
back in the East, Boston or Manhattan,
that is? I am forever still in Manila,
writing you with much concern
because the City Mayor has called
an emergency meeting to ban
the showing of all your movies,
including *Les Miserables*. The papers
and glossy fashion magazines are
christening you "Unknown," "Uncouth,"
"Uncultured," "Unconscious." Word
has it that Brooke Shields is here, too,
gambling at Heritage Casino on Roxas
with fishermen and politicians.
Is it true? Is she with André?
Are they still together? But

what you said about this city
of roaches and missing extremities
are bold impressions I cannot hold
against you, for first time travelers
from First World countries all undergo
cultural seizures here; tics
of the mind responsible for setting
off a series of generalizations
and assumptions about bugs,
blindness, and amputation. Not
excluded from this list are Filipinos
in America, like cousin Jennifer
from Daly City, Tito Bert in Wichita,
and Tita Joan in Pasadena. Claire,
I would like to invite you back
to Manila. Make another movie.
A romance, and not one filmed in a psycho
ward. Do it with Matt—Damon or
MacConaughey or Broderick, but
preferably Dillon. Or why not
Matt Mendoza, Manila's own
achy-breaky heartthrob? And bring
with you, once more, your dollars,
your talent and, this time,
crutches and roach spray.

Screening Desire

Sunday after Mass the priest behind
the screen prescribes three Our Fathers
ten Hail Marys three Glory Be's
for dropping ecstasy laced with cocaine
Friday cybersexing all night Saturday
with Hot&Horny35 from Denmark blond
blue-eyed swimmer's body in search of Asian
or Latin American bottom it must've been
his lucky night found both continents
in you as Pablo Sanchez PuertoRican
Pinoy 22 str8acting gay son of
Cultural Attaché stationed in Manila
posh bungalow brokenglasscapped subdivision
MadMax securityguards indoorpool
beachhouse in the province near a volcano
within a lake fivecar garage you drive
home to your hard drive set up
a blind date Monday evening you
and only you end up keeping Romeo23
goodlkn Moreno versatile is blaming
the rain there's flood right outside
my room I tried to reach your cellphone
says your voicemail but will try again
you forgive him you're Catholic
you wait by the phone all day Wednesday
that does not ring until Thursday
morning comes it is nobody special only
your mother asking for fashion advice
Madame Imelda's 75th birthday bash
at Manila Hotel go minimalist you say
Prada or SoEn you blast Madonna
as Evita Perón right out of your Cityland
condo studio 14 square meters reboot
the PC replace five pounds of beerbelly
with sixpack abs nice smoothchest
hung a George Michael goatee
you christen yourself not Mark

17

that was earlier this week
not John that was last week what's left?
two options Luke17 cute
afterschooldaddy bicurious cyber
phone okay or Matthew37 6'1 brwnhair
hazeleyes Italian FilAm from Big Apple
will be visiting in two weeks you
compromise and enter the chatroom as
Paul26 into 69 top please no fems or
drags a macho ritual you picked up along
with lying to please the glare
of the screen that answers back
right away from ReadyEddie Chinito
30 5'10 160 lbs bottom discreet you
score big he's a banker with high
interest in designer labels and French
cuisine let's hook up dinner first
at Le Soufflé maybe last full showing
at Glorietta4 or Starbucks for Frappuccino
you'll know him by the Emporio Armani
spreadwinged golden eagle logo across
his chest he'll spot you by your thousand
peso Paris runway haircut DKNY blk shirt
Hugo Boss stretch pants containing
chocolateflavored Trust condoms
and free samples of Astroglide lube
distributed by a non-governmental
organization in Ermita just in case
2 a.m. Saturday strikes with another
round of Jose Cuervo Gold tequila
shots at Giraffe his American
Express corporate card picks up the tab
you know he says I've never been with
a poet and gives you the most beautiful
smile in history then vanishes forever
as if to say ReadyEddie has left
the room or is simply ignoring you.

ESL, or English as a Sign Language

ALLOWANCE 70: Airline regulation for maximum weight of a *balikbayan* box.
BURGER QUEEN.
CHICKS O'CLOCK: Girlie bar a block away from Pasay City Hall.
DON'T DARE ME: Motto of action hero-turned-president Joseph Estrada.
ELIZABETH TAILORING.
FORBIDDEN TO PISS, DUMP TRASH, SHIT ON THIS WALL: 300 peso fine.
GO WITH GOD, NOT WITH DRUGS.
HEAVEN'S GATE MEMORIAL PARK.
IF ALONE, SHARE A SEAT & WIN A FRIEND: Taped on tables of Burger Queen.
JAPAYUKI FOR HIRE: Overseas employment agency recruiting (bar hostesses) to Japan.
KAREN CARPENTRY: Also accepts laundry on Sundays.
LOOKING FOR SEWERS: Hanging on glass door of Elizabeth Tailoring.
MAKE THE DEAD SMILE: Sells affordable caskets.
NO PARKING IN THE DRIVEWAY.
O, DIVA: A gay-frequented karaoke bar.
PETAL ATTRACTION: A florist right next to Edgar Scissorhands Hair & Beauty Salon.
QUIET MUST BE OBSERVED, PRAYER IN SESSION.
RESORT FOR LIFE: A retirement plan.
STAIRWAY TO HEAVEN: A mortuary.
THE PHILIPPINES IS THE ONLY ENGLISH-SPEAKING CATHOLIC COUNTRY IN ASIA. Beneath it: BEWARE OF PICK-POCKETERS.
U-TURN AROUND: A dead-end street.
VIDEOKE RENT TO OWN: Sells pirated CDs and Louis Vuitton bags made in Korea.
WALK WITH GOD, NOT WITH GUYS: Born-again Christians against teen pregnancy.
X-PORT M-PORT, CALL FOR FREE COUNSELING: For legal overseas contract worker.
YOUR BASIC KNEAD BAKERY.
ZENAIDA FERNANDEZ, Licensed Midwife. Also does home delivery.

The Superstar Talks to Her Award-Winning Role, Flor Contemplacion

It was a miracle to find us all in one movie, Flor.
National Artist for Literature Orlando Cortez
set aside his poetry and Brecht translations
to play your father. Stage actor Johnny Dizon
played your two-timing husband. Roberta Fuentes
abandoned her Visayan accent and migrated north
to Laguna to be his *querida*. But, even years
before reporters gave them column space
and prime time slots, their cake-and-eat-it-too
affair was an open-market knowledge
fat with explosive details like fishes
caught by dynamite fishing. Teen idol
Gina Moreno gained weight to play your daughter,
and my real-to-reel-life son, JonJon, signed up
for acting lessons from his award-winning
father to play Middle Child. Your own flesh-
and-blood twins, Dingdong and RhenRhen,
who called you mother once every two years
when you returned home to drop off their toys
in Duty Free bags, also appeared in the film,
hired to play themselves. Queen of Twilight
Soap, Amy de Castro, made a cameo appearance,
the most expensive ever in Filipino film history,
playing nanny to newcomer child actor Jay-R Munoz
who, in a lunchtime variety show contest,
beat out five hundred other Montessori kids
to play Ricky, the five-year-old epileptic son
of a Singaporean couple who started it all
when he had a seizure and drowned in a bathtub
swollen with rubber duckies. I was in

Daly City, California, performing *Domestic
Violence*, a one-woman show based on the plight
of Filipina maids overseas, when my director/
agent/confidant Kristian Montenegro
hand-delivered me Rimbaud Woo's script. Tita,

Kristian said, this is our ticket back to Cannes.
During filming I discovered Rimbaud had
spilled out your life in one night while suffering
from delirium caused by dengue fever and
imported diet pills from Bangkok. Rimbaud,
thank god, survived the four o'clock mosquitoes.
According to "The Buzz" with Kris Aquino and
Ricky Lo, Rimbaud is now working on the sequel.

The bio-pic contained the usual secret
ingredients for international film festival entries:
slap-and-shout dialogue, extra-and-ordinary scenes
requiring only my eyes to speak. There is
an interrogation scene complete with yellow
subtitles between me and Singaporean officials,
played by Chinese-Filipino-looking extras
who raped me until I confessed to a crime
committed by water. And before I forget
the month-long wake attended by media,
presidential hopefuls, feminists, U.P. activists,
human rights victims, maids returning from
or destined for Bahrain, United Emirates, Sydney,

Hong Kong. To complete the list of mourners,
the unforgettable Matronas de Metro Manila who,
in ballroom gowns and Benzes driven by
their tango instructors, went straight to the wake
after coming from a formal-wear-only occasion
celebrating the grand opening of Starbucks
in Makati. Most difficult part to film was,
to our surprise, not the tear-and-rope-jerking
execution scene nor the it's-all-in-the-eyes
dialogue between me, my children, and a sound-
and-bullet-proofed glass, but getting former
President Ramos to re-memorize his three-
minute televised speech, asking the public to please
pray for the departing soul of Flor Contemplacion.
After fifty-two takes, ex-Prez nailed it.
Lucky for Gina. She was starting to have anxiety
attacks and acne breakouts over not completing
the film in time for her next bio-pic on Sarah

Balabagan, Filipina Muslim teenster who lied
about her age so she could maid in the Middle East,
post-Gulf War, for an Arab she ended up butchering
in self-defense. Amazingly, we completed
filming in two weeks, one week ahead of schedule
and just in time for the Metro Manila Film
Festival where we took home awards in all
categories, including Best Parade Float.

Manila, My Manila: Wish List For a Day

Clear-cut directions to get me
To the public restrooms on time;

Toilets with seats
Or toilet seats without beads of piss;

An entrée from the menu
Or one that won't make me turn yellow.

Shit, oh, shit,
Help me shit in peace and order.

McDonald's without gun-crazed guards,
Spaghetti minus the sugar,

Cup of water that won't give me the runs;
Long-lost aunts who don't pimp their daughters;

Three rounds of guilt-free sex
With a bottom Born-Again Christian,

A top Catholic Charismatic,
And a versatile Muslim rebel wanted by Colonel Powell.

Also, for the Virgin Mary to take a day off
From apparitions and infomercials.

Ave, Ave, Ave Maria,
Have mercy and free her for a day.

Cardiac-friendly horns,
Motorists to brake for pedestrians,

President Arroyo to make an Anime
About a city that sinks under the heat and swims in the rain.

Sidewalks that don't drop to Hades,
And travel-friendly roads to bring me back to your kiss.

If I a Gay

No way. But if I a gay
I have no way out but death or think,
Okay, fine, I a gay, go crazy, it's normal,
Shoot the president of Our Lady
Of Perpetual Help High School senior class
Because homosexuality to his snake eyes
Is lonely and acceptable only inside sin asylum.
At his wake, jockmates itch with tears,
The virgins of his lucky dreams dry up,
His parents in denial for forty days.
But I know they be first to thank me
For the two bullets in their son's head,
If they find out he was also a gay
With many sunrise-sunset boyfriends who give him China
For breakfast, make out business signs
Like: WE QUEER, YOU HEAR?,
Spot him out in the gym, and spend
His allowances on opera tickets, Norwegian
Cruisers, White-Only parties, Camel-hair
Coats, foreign film DVDs, ecstasy pills.

If I a gay, right away I become role model
For other working-class gays who want go prom
With many other gays. We all slow dance,
Lovey-dovey-like for news cameramen and
White House. The angry President
Interrupt Prime-Time and make wars again.
Anybody with my eyes or nose get arrested.
Everyone in my family tree get deported
Back to watermelon islands, and the Marines
Chop-chop my long-leggedness
If I don't make underground on time.
I might or might not if I a gay.

Rhapsody

Eh, Cedric, no look now
But the guy at five o'clock stay ogling us.
That's the vocab word for tonight.
Means: Eyes fondling us.
The guy over there getting ritas on Bloody Mary,
The one trying hard for hold his pickle straight.
I think he like do you or me or us both.

Mahalo nui loa, but no thanks.
He just another Midwest clone with one Savannah perm.
National Geographic should do one documentary
On haoles who look like Billy Ray Cyrus, yeah?
Goin' win one award at the Cannes, you watch.

Is that the twins Carl and Lance Nakashima?
Try look them.
McKinley-high-grad Japs feeling *high-makamaka*.
2-4-1 double-eye operations that came with color contacts.
They think they all dis'n'dat,
Throwing one-mile-per-hour attitude left and right
In their DKNYs and Kenneth Cole boots. Pah-lease.
Bet you they bought 'em incognito at the Waikele outlet,
Along with the *boboras* from Nagoya and Osaka.

Oh. My. God.
Brad? Braderick Alohakakahiaka Peterson, is that you?
Thanks, you look great yourself.
Northwest?
Base for good or just laying over?
Narita?
Class Reunion?
Room 602?
Ahui ho.

Only in his dreams, Cedric.
You think I go back for sloppy seconds?
No doubt the sky-slut get one oversized carry-on
But the thing stay all covered with cheese.

Speaking of fromage…Francois,
Can have another round of screaming orgasm?
Scratch the cherry
And, eh, no need be stingy with the Kal.lua.
Merci beaucoup.
Eh, Cedric, thought for tonight:
If Versace never designed such loud clothes
You think he would've attracted Andrew Cunanan?
Poor serial-killer social-climber fame-sponger,
Finally made it to CNN
And the reporters couldn't even pronounce his name.
Pah-lease. No more "Q" in his name and then.

Turn to two o'clock in one minute.
Yeah, that's Tony.
Or should I say Antonio Macadangdang Macaraeg?
The *momona manong* from Moanalua High.
Blow job Queen of Kapiolani Park who
Drops more names than *Entertainment Tonight* and
Wayne Harada's column combined.
Did you know he wen' change his name to Toni Cortez?
Toni with an "I"?
Yeah, ever since *Miss Saigon* time, the touring company.

Oh, you in *Les Miz* now, Toni?
Sorry, cannot keep up with you nowadays.
You in Madonna's new video?
Ricky Martin, too?
Wow, we impressed.
We impressed, yeah, Cedric?
Anna and the King too?
Jodie Foster?
You and Jodie real close?
Really?
For real?

Look what the stroke of midnight brought in.
Somfong Xayapeth, F.O.B. from Highwater Pants, Laos,
And sugar baby to Immigration Officer Shrock.
Look the way they stay tonguing each other.
Real *moe lepo*, them two.

Real public display of disgrace.
I feel like I reliving the water buffalo-
Slaughtering scene in *Apocalypse Now*.
Freakin' gross.
Eh, Francois, *hayaku* with the drinks already.

Tita Aida

I. The Almighty

If the fever does not go away, fasten your seat belts, girlfriends, and wait for Saint Jude to cross your legs. If he takes too long, sweep your thoughts together and call the Hotline. No charge, girlfriends, and the voices you hear are real. Tell 'em about the chills, night sweats, and runs you've been having. Open your palms and read to 'em the expeditions you took, how many, and where. Don't forget to mention any shipwrecks, perished pilots, and moss growing on your skin. When those closet doors swung open and spit froze in our eyes, did we whimper and make a U-turn? No, girlfriends, we flexed our muscles and painted our nails suck-me violet. Then we took a blowtorch and burnt the damn closet to thy kingdom come. Not my kingdom, but theirs, girlfriends, the ones over there with the jasmine crucifix and fornicating beards. The first few nights are always the hardest. The spiking fever, delirious lips, and skin so dry you could peel it off and make sandwich bags. But, like catechism and singles bars, you'll get used to it and begin to take it as it is without asking why no one comes up to you anymore and hands over a calling card with a name written in magic marker. You'll even learn how to float without tire tubes or air mats. So hang in there, girlfriends, and the vines will surely get to you. Grow your hair a few inches longer and you'll feel like Rapunzel, abandoned, but still waiting pretty. Remember: think straight and the voices you hear are real. Don't wait too long for Jude because he might be on vacation and won't be able to find your lungs by the time he asks you to breathe deep and hold.

II. The Father

Stop calling me Dad because I stopped being your father ever since you sashayed out of this house in your ringlets and bobby pins and corset or whatever you call it. I can't even think right because everyone wants to know who put those purple spots between your ass. Don't look at me as if you never asked for it either because you had yourself all ready for anyone who tripped on your satin gown. Some satin trick. Think I didn't know what you were doing behind my back? Stop pretending that you're sorry because you loved every minute of it. Should've been there when you had heaven groped so I could record it and play it for you. So stop giving me this drama crap and don't even dare think for a second that I'm gonna touch you. Won't need to. All I have to do is breathe on you and you'll be out of here. Look at this, finally make the front page and you had to share it with a hundred other people. Front page with colored picture and all, they mixed you up with another guy and got your name spelled wrong. Even yakked about the first one. Conspiring under the mango tree with a married man. You make me sick. You better shut up. Better yet, get up and go tell 'em how you invented everything. Put a map over your body and call it sacrifice. Get up and show 'em how you stood in the dark and never got enough.

III. The Son

He is a picture spoiled by the rain that enters through the wooden slats. I remember his face when Mercy comes over for siesta to write the date and my name on the wall. Only three rusty nails, but so many thorns. When I go, forget pounding nails through these palms. Got enough blood jetting out from every hole of this body. Just tell me to spit and I'll fill up a milk bottle. Kiss the thorns goodbye because I got enough headache to last me for the afterlife. I wish I were Mercy who's pumping-iron strong and used to lead when I wanted to cha cha cha the boring afternoon away. I don't dance anymore, gave up on the beat, threw my arms and legs to the monkey bar forever. I just swallow capsules and watch Mercy put numbers and words on the wall. When I go, she promised to paint my nails soft-shell red and dress me up in a beaded gown, my runway gown, and pin a tiara made from mango leaves. I love Mercy. She taught me how to peel the blue strips off the capsules and save them for souvenirs. They make fantastic ribbons. Indigo for rainy nights. Turquoise for summer solstice. Electric blue for fiesta dances. She keeps them in an old biscuit tin under the broken phonograph stand. When she wipes the siesta sweat off me and takes my temperature, I remember his face and Mercy starts to make up the past. Me in golden curls and pink muscle-T. Patty-cake, patty-cake, sores and shakes, nobody else but me. Cha cha, cha cha cha, it's flaming hot and nobody else but me. I love Mercy and think Mercy and she keeps her promise, soft-shell red because I remember the picture, indigo because it's a rainy night, mango-leaf tiara and a beaded gown. I pull my tongue out and tie tie the words and numbers around my tongue, indigo, and cha cha cha and tie tie tie and pull hard and tight, again and again and again for souvenir, baby, for souvenir.

Says the Kiwi Bird

The poet does not know what to do with me.
It has come down to this, unfortunately.

At eight o'clock, he switches channels
And enters the yellow doorframe of *National Geographic*.

Just when the all-day rain is beginning
To show signs of drying up for the night,

He skims through his memory saved on dinner napkins
Then studies the rectangle of a window.

He is praying for help.
I know this for a fact.

He wants to write me off
Before the winged ants of Northern Luzon come.

A female voiceover from New Zealand
Is put in charge of delivering him all the facts.

She performs her duties well, I must say.
Always on cue, in sync with the footage.

In case her accent fails to reach him
There are, for backup, yellow subtitles in Chinese.

According to the English language, we are not size-conscious;
It is the length of our bills that give away our gender.

We measure no more than an embrace, burrow in six-foot
Tunnels, walk with our backs hunched to the night.

True: We are birds without wings
But this is not why we are falling in numbers.

Aside from being meat for the hungry,
We provide plumage for collectors and work for taxidermists.

Our talent ranges from crying for miles
To smelling worms buried under inches of dirt.

What else?
Oh, yes, we lay eggs the shape of prehistory.

The Maoris include us chief among their diet
Which we accept, being part of Nature's buffet.

Our entrance into the White Man's world was like that
Of indigenous tribes: We existed only in his imagination.

For we, too, are brown and live in bush-covered homes.
But let me ask the poet and any of you who have seen us:

Do we look anything at all like penguins?
Do we wear tuxedos and skate on ice?

Do we carry umbrellas?
Are there comic strips starring us?

What a crime! This is enough to make us join Orwell's revolution.
One Imagist even had the gall to call us emus.

Why? Because we inhabit the same continent?
Emus are dinosaurs, for bill's sake.

When push comes to shove
We dig tunnels in a blink and are ready to fight

And die for the territory of our souls.
Oh, I can go on and on. I won't, though.

The poet is desperate and needs my help.
A migration of winged ants has invaded the room

Of mood swings and invention, and, like moths,
Try to find solace in a clean and well-lighted home

That will eventually shed them one by one
Until the poet is showered with fallen wings

Instead of laurels.
Such is the ritual of a bright killing.

I know I am only a kiwi bird
(Okay, a poet's muse for the first time tonight)

But I do understand the laws of territoriality:
Nuisance, and, above all, creation.

This Poem Is Called "Waiting" or "The Problems of Using Metaphors In Confessional Poetry"

If I have to explain to you
line by line what the poem
is about, whether the image
of the hard rain in line four
is nothing more than a windward shower,
or me dropping torrential hints
about an illicit affair with
a thespian while you were stranded
on the "Freeway of Love" which
is the Aretha Franklin song
that appears in the first stanza

If you have to explain to me
how you piece the poem together,
that reading is nothing more than
an act of getting inside my head,
of unscrambling my feelings,
of decoding my thoughts, intentional
or not, by equating, for example,
the actor to an assistant professor
who isn't from LA but in DC
where the MLA conference took place
earlier this year, and we both know
this because our friend Tina,
PhD in Restoration Lit, flew there
to be interviewed for several tenure-
track positions, and though there's
no mention of Tina anywhere
in the poem, you say it makes more
sense to change the title "Waiting"
to "Job Hunt" and still end
up with seven letters

What if we set aside poetry
and go to the movies instead,

as we did in the beginning,
relaxing on my second-hand couch,
munching microwave popcorn and
holding hands throughout *TNT Salutes
The Oscars*, our clasp tightening
when Beatrice Straight, who won
an Oscar for a five-minute role
in the kitchen (talk about
supporting!), asked her husband,
played by William Holden, if he,
after twenty-five years of marriage,
was in love with another woman,
Faye Dunaway, and he, knowing what
she already knew, said yes, because
Faye made him feel alive ouch

Isn't this what drove those Greek
philosophers to hemlock and American
Top-40 poets to broken-record
breakdowns: devoting an entire life
and savings, asking where did their love
go when they already had the answers?

On Days That Break Us

On days that break us
when we have no one to hold
or no one to hold us,
except for a handful of words
we are still getting used to,

the door slamming on us
whenever we talk back
or stories coming back
we find hard to believe
or don't have words for,

on days like today
when we have no words
to give us our daily breath
or Sunday bread to break,
my dear friend, I find you

on the pages of my prayers
slightly short of miracles
these past few months, I am afraid,
a traffic jam at the most,
or if I am lucky, a seeing-eye dog,

reminding me of small miracles
that with smaller miracles
have brought me this far thus far
when the most important things I say
are the first broken sounds I make.

Slippery When English

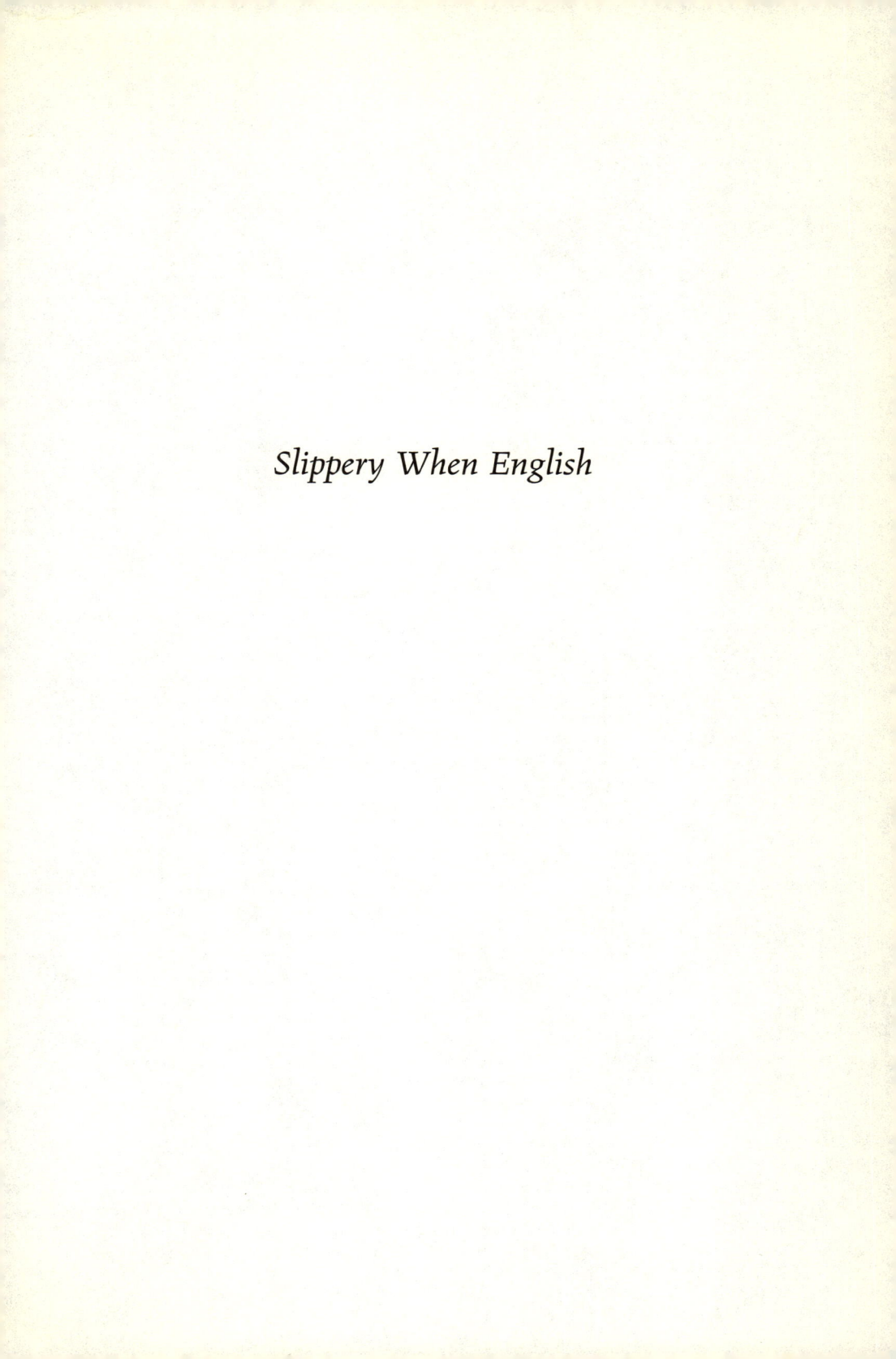

After Carl Dreyer's *Ordet (The Word)*

I.

We need more than caffeine
To convince our brother
Johannes that he is not Jesus,
But a somnambulist passing
White windblown sheets
On his way to the sand dunes.
Every morning, he greets us
With "I am only a bricklayer,
But no one lives in my house."

"Too much Kierkegaard," our
Father says, "and he wasn't
Even studying to become a pastor."
Poor Johannes.
The price he pays
For his addiction to books.

When he isn't lighting candles
And placing them on the east
And west of a windowsill,
He's writing us quotes from
Saint John of the Cross, tucking
Our little niece to bed, collapsing
After he says "Arise!" and
Disrupting talks on marriage
To deliver messages like:
"I see a corpse in the living room,"
"Woe unto you if you nail me again,"
And our favorite, "There he goes again,
The man with the hourglass."

Once, he frightened the new pastor,
A young, handsome man who believes
Only in old miracles. "Your son…
Is he…How did he…shouldn't he be…

Was it a love affair?" "No," Father
Said, "Soren."
And left it at that.

II.

"Knowledge comes from experience,"
"Truth is subjective,"
"Religion is based on you,"
Are all we know of Soren Kierkegaard,
But it was enough to change
Our ways of reading and believing.

III.

To prepare Preben Lerdoff Rye for the role of Johannes, the theology scholar who goes insane from speculations, doubts, and Kierkegaard's "Live what you believe in" doctrines, Carl Dreyer, the Danish filmmaker who directed *The Passion of Joan of Arc*, drives him one afternoon to a mental institution because he wants the young actor to experience what it's like living in a room with a door that has no handle. He wants to familiarize him with the architecture of entrapment: What it's like to step inside a box with only a shaft of light dividing day from night; the purpose to heighten claustrophobia and, in turn, magnify the desire to escape. The stronger the desire is, the narrower the walls become. The brighter the light, the darker the hours. Pointing his finger past the window, Dreyer tells Preben, "To Johannes, there is no difference between this room and that sky."

The second purpose for their visit is more intimate: Dreyer wants Preben to meet the patient he once thought of casting. The patient introduces himself to the director and actor. "I am an artist," he says, his speech slow, methodical, perfectly measured, as if each breath requires a frame to itself. Preben falls silent, his eyes fixed on the man's face. Years later, in a documentary on Dreyer's life and works, Preben, sitting in a room not much brighter than the patient's, describes Dreyer as the "most beautiful portrait of Jesus Christ on the Cross."

IV.

It is common knowledge in the celluloid world that Dreyer is a firm believer in method acting. But he doesn't preach it or Stanislavsky to the actors. He prefers to tell them jokes, scold them for wearing makeup, take them shopping for stockings or leave them tied to a cross while he goes to the canteen for lunch. If he's in a good mood, he'll say, "Bring the corpse up to the canteen and feed him in his coffin."

Based on a play by Kaj Monk, *The Word*, starring Preben Lerdoff Rye in the role of Johannes/Jesus, was released internationally in 1954 and became one of Dreyer's most popular films.

V.

Whose side is Faith on?
The tailor?
The farmer?

A Modest Manila Proposal

Seven-letter word for a metropolitan python
that digests patience and excretes death wish
see also bumper-to-bumper gridlock drive-
amok aggressive-regressive door-to-door
throw in pollution too since we're on a roll
potholes the size of Mars and Metro Rail
Transit to be completed *mañana*
and like tomorrow it begins with a "T"
with jam and brake and ends this crossword
puzzle of a city with me as its hostage
buckled to a car seat still sealed in plastic
like my Tita Baby's imported couch and
Philippine passport unlimited entry
to Disneyland and Universal Studios thank you
both stashed in her barbed-wire subdivision
home the Akyat-Bahay gang once climbed into
to burglarize the laser karaoke machine
portrait of Christ with a bleeding heart and
Santo Niño also sealed in plastic why these three
specifically and not the pyramid cans
of Hormel corned beef Folgers coffee
displayed in the living room in a glass cabinet
with 24-hour alarm why these three nobody knows
and to tell you frankly nobody gives
the burglars bade adieu, planted Marlboro-
stained kisses on the Visayan maids
who blossomed nine months later approximately

the same time it is taking me to get
to my blind date, from Makati Ave to Megamall
via EDSA this is enough to start a highway
revolution or a coup d'état don't you agree
a friend, a fan of Steven Seagal's action-
packed movies, suggested planting explosives
at rail transit and skyway construction sites
another came up with the idea of doing
what that Chinese businessman did years

back which is simply to drive down
a one-way street one hand firing a machine
gun to impress everyone who controls
the traffic light that works only when it wants to
once a friend of a friend planned the perfect
murder of his ex-pat of an ex
during a three-hour gridlock
will you please shut her up please I tell
the cabbie whose name and face are laminated
and clipped onto the visor next to
my reflection she gives me migraine
anxieties too I say and Celine Dion
disappears into the romantic Titanic void
thank you I say and fish for my Xanax
pop five five-milligram pills I want to break

here and say not all traffic jams lead to funeral
parlors five-star hotels prison cells rehab
there exist non-violent ways of crushing
Philippines' worst nightmare of the century
third only to foreign invasions and the Marcoses
like Gandhi I too am an advocate for Nobel Peace
Prize worship the pink habits of Carmelite Sisters
and admire of Corazon Aquino and all her
TIME's Woman-of-the-Year yellowness and in crisis
such as this sandwiched between a jeepney named
Salvacion and a hand-me-down bus from Japan
go figure go Sony go back to World War II
but no I choose instead to return to literature
and make peace with European novelists
creators of term papers and yesterday's epic
buried in Paris with rock stars and Modigliani
yesterday it was a truce with Tolstoi and *Anna K*
the day before *Les Miz* the Hugo version
and not the musical or the Liam Neeson film flop
last week was a bumpy journey with
one of the Karamazovs along the road construction
of Aurora Boulevard *Notes From the Underground*

to be exact which is what this city is becoming
I recommend you do the same take my advice

to heart especially if you enjoy translations
and me-myself-and-I-encountering-the-Other
narratives like Conrad's *Heart of Darkness* which
I read from cover to cover foreword by Joyce Carol
Oates included in three blocks without
interruption except to buy a paper bag of garlic-
seasoned peanuts true the novella was slim
but the horror the horror was right outside
the tinted window no change of view from
the day before same hollow-blocked jungle
overpopulated by Swift's children whose fingers
were ringed with jasmine leis competing against
blind amputees for over-the-window
third-world coins and right behind them tall
brown and handsome commercial model Paolo Bediones
and Kurtz weaving in and out of traffic pushing
a *Palmolive*-sponsored portable sink on wheels
offering to shampoo condition then hot oil
the heads stuck in traffic for free.

Slippery When English

You're barking up the wrong dog, Your Honor.
How many times do I have to repeat my testament?
I told you it was a standing-in-the-room only.
Yes, I've been there, been that; that I won't deny.
But there was a blessing in those guys.
I couldn't just turn my blind eyes.
Yes, I usually did the slamming doors, Your Honor.
Usually due to excruciating circumstances,
Or too many excess luggage from the past.
Of course, I thought hard about it.
It's not always easy come, easy goes, you know.
It's at the back of my head the whole time, too.
But I am a thief of risks.
I love the "cha" in "challenge."
Besides, who's going to lift their fingers for me?
Only the devil can do his own job, right?
Otherwise, what good is passion without a pitchfork?
If that's the case, "p" in "punishment" should not be capitalized.
So cut me some slacks, Your Honor.
I told you it was an accident.
He popped the question; I jumped the gun.
It was a no win-win situation.
I thought he was only shooting breezes.
He turned out to be dead serious.
That's what I've been trying to tell you, your Honor:
You can never *can* tell.
It either happens or it doesn't.
Or you think it does but not really.
Or it's not real.
Do I think I'll fall again?
I don't know.
That's a pretty tight spot to be in.
Let's just say I'll burn the bridge when I get there.
Yes, Your Honor, love sure is a crazy planets.
But that's not my problem anymore;
That's your problem anymore.
So please, Your Honor, do not judge me.
I am not a book.

And Yet

I am tired of communing with the walls, lobbying for metaphors,
　　flirting with the blizzard;
Of breaking even, getting even, Wallace Stevens.
This morning, my horoscope said, "Go back to night school, major
　　in auto mechanics, and minor in Gregg's shorthand."
What have I to lose?
Wrestling with the angels doesn't excite me anymore.
And the demons? They can have their dream back.
My Alexandria is up for grabs; the blueprint is in the shower.
I am through, too, through explaining to my mother why my
　　paycheck never exceeds two digits, to my lovers why Neruda
　　weeps over barbershops, to my shrink why Sylvia Plath keeps
　　popping out of the oven.
No more, thank you.
Here on, it's goodbye to bread line, inspiration quota, and two
　　complimentary copies plus a year's subscription at 50% off;
Goodbye to putting Lorca into Creole, substituting macadamia nuts
　　for olives.
No more sautéing my liver in liquor, horse-pissing with O'Neil,
　　going overboard with Crane, that tragic babe.
No more latenight "Stein or Joyce?" catfights.
Clear the shelves, except the *Collected Poems of Frank O'Hara*,
　　edited by Donald Allen; that one I bought new on eBay.
And, like Akhmatova, kill memory, kill time, especially the time I
　　took up yoga at the Y taught by a haole Tibetan Buddhist, my
　　early nineties crush, and the paramedics had to pry me out of
　　the lotus.
No more seventy revisions of "Portraits of Desire."
Bid adieu to cubbyhole therapy with Dostoevsky, breathing lessons
　　with Chekhov.
Beginning today, no more doing it for love, hunger, self-help.
Beginning today, it's darkness with insurance, meditation with
　　guaranteed Nirvana.

Why Cicadas Have More Fun

You're probably wondering where I'm going with this
I wish I could tell you
I, too, am waiting
They're not around very often, only every seventeen years; hence
    their first name, *Periodical,*
That's how long it takes them to break out of the underworld and
    see the White House through vermilion eyes
The males have only four weeks to sing, hook up,
    and fulfill their Bug-given duties
Then they become bad buffet in the food chain
If you never heard them sing, imagine bugs buzzing a million
    different buzz notes a minute
The females live an extra week to cut into trees and lay their
    legacy that, in six weeks, will hatch, and a million nymphs
    will burrow underground
Until it's time to strip, buzz, fuck, die, make sidewalks slippery,
    and give cats and dogs constipation.

The Muse This Time

I am, at the moment, a patron of the meat market. Profession: a poet on call because poetry only comes when it wants to; hobbies: listening to Gershwin while looking for Freud in Woody Allen movies; history of the heart: six lovers who wanted to be immortalized.

"Funny," said my fourth, "you can cook up a poem about bumper-to-bumper traffic, but when it's time to write about me…." How do you explain to someone who makes you come thrice a week and gives you head and foot massage at bedtime why it is much easier to write about gridlock in the land of diesel than return to that humid night in Makati, where we had met, in a Korean-owned steam room, a misnomer since lust provided the heat.

The fifth and sixth were more demanding. "Screw the acknowledgment page," said the fifth. "I want a biography that sings," said the sixth. Completely unaware they were making the same request an hour apart from each other. I told them, "What do you take me for? A mail-order poet? Dial-a-Poem?"

"I don't get it," said the third, "you can create beauty from a dead fish, and destroy buildings in one line, but you cannot write about the good ole devil?"

Their words are stinging now as I approach twilight. Truth is: love's hard to live with. I forget to set the alarm clock, I buy everything on credit, I start making up words, I call in sick to the world. "Are you a poet?" asked the second. "A lover?" asked the third. "Just shut up and write," said the first.

I can't. Nothing is entering. Except the voice of my first, the one who set the picture straight. "The problem with you is you think you're Woody Allen in *Manhattan*."

Gershwin's blue clarinet, black-and-white Big Apple, an ice cream parlor. At the counter, Woody is buying Hemingway's granddaughter, Mariel, a milkshake before he delivers the bad news. Tears coursing down her cheeks, she asks, "Why? Because I'm too young? Because I don't know Rita Hayworth from Veronica Lake?

Because I'm not Diane Keaton running with you in the rain?" They split, then a minute before the credits roll, he changes his mind. "I'll take you back," Mariel says, "when I return from London."

That's the closest to my idea of love: watching the skyline, making out, making mistakes, making believe desire means it's with somebody else, then breaking up, and, if we're lucky, forgiveness that comes right before takeoff. There, I've said it. What more can one want? A lover who loves me as much as rain. Rain and, from the opening credits to the closing heart, Gershwin.

Moo

I. In a Sentimental Moo

First, it was yesterday's lawn mower
Cutting into my dream-chase sleep.

Today, it was the greatest hits of
And performed by the Moo family.

I thought I tuned everything out.
Last one to clear out was Prokofiev.

I was wrong.
As the all-day conference

Was about to kick off,
Pen and paper handy for the artist

(Impressive word—"artist,"
Means "maker from nothing"

Or "milker of everything"),
The Moo chorale began

Their dress rehearsal with
"In a Sentimental Moo,"

Followed by "I Moo It from the Grapevine,"
Then "Come on, Feel the Moos,"

A heavy metal number loaded
With horn-banging refrains.

To cool things down, Queen
Mootifah took center corral

With "Killing Me Softly with His Moo"
Before the special guests,

All the way from Mu'u Mu'u islands,
Gave it their Polynesian all

With "Pearly Moos."
"Memory Moo" was next,

A rock ballad that reminded me
Of my old remedial English days:

What did blank-blank have on his farm?
Which God's creature jumped over His what?

For encore, "Blue Moo,"
A classic standard at the end of the day

Made everyone wish
For an "N."

II. Dial "M" for Moo

How dare you stand there wide-eyed?
Go and Moo somebody else's field.

Why seek inspiration from us?
Go ask the birds.

III. What the Cows Taught Me About Etymology

Day starts by listening, observing,
Praying to the four squares of light

Then darkness—rough,
But necessary—slams.

The book opens
And there you are:

Listed under "cattle,"
Related to "chattel" and "capital."

Makes sense you're all about money.
Pecuniary which

Latins tells us
Comes from *pecus*, cattle.

You descended from the aurochs,

(*Bos primigenius*), wild ox

Of Europe, now extinct,
Chased out of the woods

By bullets
And falling trees.

Some claim you're European from Moo to toe,
Others argue Asia.

The purist is black Angus.
The shaggy red is Hereford.

Now and then,
A white face will show up.

That's what happens
When red and black bump.

As for the dairy:
Jerseys buttered through and through.

Regardless of origin,
Be proud. Oprah fought for you and won.

Had Bush, Texas, and a good chunk
Of the stock market fuming for months.

Julius Caesar wrote about your modesty,
Columbus, the second time around,

Brought you in his Ark
to the Second World.

You probably know all this,
Embarrassed to say, I didn't.

But now do.
Thanks to your hullabaloo Moo.

Caliban's Epilogue

It's true: he no could believe
First time he saw me.
I not in his books, that's why.
He had to make me up.
"Clay-lump," "hag-seed"—
Any kind names for give me form.
When he patient, I his "Tortoise,"
When he not, I his "Sloth!"
To others, I either one fish or spotted dog.
In short, not human.

Twelve years ago,
He gave me language
For separate moon from sun,
Daughters from dukes,
Music from beast.

Twelve years ago,
He gave me home;
His cave, my bed.

Fast I learned about power.
Fast I learned desire punishment.
I never had choice: his daughter
Slept in the cave, too.

Twelve years I was his slave.
His music I cursed
His curses I made my poetry,
When I wasn't making fire,
Or watching him spy
On lovers, like my father before.

Now, he giving up,
No like rule this island no more.
He rather be prisoner in his body.

The magic, the music, the air
stay leaving already.
Except me,
Me, Caliban, heir to exile.

First Lessons

Remember this: humans lie, chickens lay.
Avoid words like "oozing" because everything
oozes not only blood but love and lust.
Put aside Carver and Bukowski
for the meantime; that rum and Coke too.
They'll resurface like all the others,
the way Dickens' ghost returns each December
or Hamlet's father whenever darkness
drops in from nowhere. Pay attention instead
to the walls of your apartment building
and record the landlady who nightly quizzes
her husband on how well he knows her, what
color her panties were on their wedding
night, the number of orgasms she simulated.
Eavesdrop, cheat, lie, peep, argue, document.
It's a war, yes, and if you begin to feel
lost and uncertain why suddenly your eyes
are breathing as the earth does after
a morning rain, or during a fight with
a lover the f-word blossoms into a dozen
roses, that means you're onto something
larger than metaphor, meaning you're
on a map in the making. By this, I don't
mean navigating the seven clichéd seas or
horseback-riding the Alamo with Wayne
gunning down Mexicans and tomahawks trained
by Hollywood to feign their deaths. Pursue,
attack, seduce, and yes, like the Marcoses,
steal, steal everything and more. Loot,
horde, storm the Palace of Spines and rearrange
Dewey, the canons and the classics of tomorrow
too. Just remember: in poetry there is
only one cardinal rule practiced by all: steal
with the intent to replace. This and, yes,
don't rush. You still have a poem to write.

Academia 101

I'm sorry, Sir, the documents
your byline depends on
are now in the hands of war,

fire, and other grant-dependent
fellows like yourself, who make
a habit of returning here

to their doctoral roots to collect
anthropomorphic plants, track
down 16th-century carvings

of saints with lopped-off
noses, or climb the 8th golden
wonder of the world

with ex-headhunters to shoot
facsimiles of turn-of-the-century
hand-painted photographs,

such as that of American anthropologist
Dean Worcester looking very dignified
beside two warriors in G-strings,

shouldering a bamboo pole
from which hangs
a body without a head. However,

not all scholars are trapped
in their private mini-museums
or driven wild by exotic low-budget

dreams. There are those, for example,
who do not take offense at the way
we drive amok, form multiple lines

from a single line, talk nonstop
to Nokia throughout *Lord of the Rings*,
reverse the way we live their metaphors.

Such challenging feats are reserved
for the likes of the Comp Lit professor
from the Midwest, who asked me,

in perfect Pilipino, why we Asians
in Asian and Asian-American fiction
are so secret-driven. I answered:

I cannot speak for the Chinese,
but you are in the country of too-many-
tongues battling to spill all at once

the secrets you Westerners prefer
to bury in print. As for the
young Fil-Am Fulbright scholar,

who came here the other day, looking
for diaries, stories, anything
penned by former students

of American teachers recruited
by McKinley in 1901 to teach and pacify
the little brown brothers with English,

apples, and snow: our stories are
not preserved in touch-sensitive cabinets,
but on tongues darker than blood,
more savage than ink.

Itinerary

Errata

The Washington Post whacks my door at
six this morning, reminding me that yesterday's
world is still on a suicide mission, making up
wars, covering boo-boos, uncovering graves,
cashing in on the X-Men, mistaking identities,
inhaling viruses, reporting something is
definitely wrong with Toni Morrison
in the sentence
"*Toni Morrison's genius
enables her to create novels that arise from
and express the injustice African Americans
have endured*"
What's wrong with Ms. Morrison
now? There are two. First, it's not a sentence;
it's question #10 for my niece Pamel, a junior
at Farrington High. Second, the multiple-choice
answer is not, as the experts claim, E,
"no error," nor D, "have endured," nor
C, "and express," nor B, "arise from."
The problem lies in:
        "her to create"—A.
This is according to a haole teacher in Maryland
Who, spotting the October error, brought his case
all the way to the front page and won a victory
for half a million students across America,
my niece included. Or not.
I think not.
Feisty as a five-month old fetus, it won't
surprise Honolulu that Pamel joined the fifty-three
percent geniuses and second guessers who did
not differentiate gender from genius. Otherwise,
she would've argued that genitals came first—
by six months.

    I remember
bombing
    big time

on the SAT verbals. How
I hated being in a panic-ridden room, shading
(with a number two pencil) bubbles to culturally-
biased questions meant more to confuse me
than measure my intellect. It was draining,
trying to make sense all morning of an English Texas
Instruments did not manufacture.
    I left my anxieties
four hours later,
   discombobulated, like a NutraSweet
gerbil, my mind still whipping the treadmill,
my TOEFL tongue tofu-thick, numbed. The boxes
second-class citizens get shoved into! Which appropriate
box should we check? We whose English will always be
used against us? How presumptuous! How
preposterous! How infinitely haole!
                     Well,
pardon my English
   for calling your "crudités" my
"pupu platter," your order of raw fish, I hate to say,
is "sashimi"—not "sushi," for preferring
to hang out in "shopping centers"—not "malls"—
or pass the day cruising through the "countryside" and
not "suburbs" with their matching walls, dogs,
and security guards, and for keeping such words as
"talk-story" and "injustice" in the plural.

A Portrait of the Poet, Smallkid Time

I.

When I was in fifth grade,
Miss K. made us write a poem
for the State Annual Poetry
Contest, Division III.

...if chosen, $100.00....

Our eyes went bonkers. Our faces
wore hundred-dollar smiles. Even
"Twinkles" Batongbacal's packed-on
makeup and "Honeygirl" Perez'
Scotch-taped eyelids were peeled
off by the crisp Ben Franklin.

...read your poem out loud...top three...

We all gave the evil-
eye to each other, thinking,
Eh, wot? You tink you one poet?
No way, Jose. I get da last word.
We walked around with an I-spit-
on-your-poem attitude, except
to Jennifer Stewart cuz she was the only one
who could speak, read, write
English right.

II.
   I told Miss K. I did not
   know what to write
      so
   she popped a quarter out.
"Here, catch the 52 Circle Island. Write
   'bout the people on the bus,
     study their faces,
    and write.
      If

>   you're
>   still stuck,
>   ask for a transfer
> and keep riding the pen."

III.

For one week, we were frustrated.
Line breaks, metaphors, similes,
haole-write English. But when sixth-
period P.E. came, we spilled out
our insecurities with sham battle,
German dodgeball, flag football,
and every ball imaginable.

IV.

When time came,
everyone went up:

    Jr. Santiago, the only Filipino who had enough courage to admit he ate black dogs, wrote 'bout   his first time at a cockfight in Waipahu.

    Edward Caraang III, wrote 'bout   coming to America and shopping at Gem's.

    Lisa Ann "Honeygirl" Perez wrote 'bout   her third time with her babe Darren.

    Frank Concepcion wrote 'bout   being an altar boy in the Philippines and the fun he had with the priests who played with him and let him sleep over.

    Cary Kaneshiro wrote 'bout   winning the Chinese Jacks competition.

    Randall Keola Lim wrote 'bout   his first time with "Honeygirl" Perez inside the big cannon in front of Fort DeRussy.

    Swee Ming "Suzanne" Low wrote 'bout   Dim Sum.

Darren Sipili wrote 'bout   beefing Randall after school.

Kalani "Babes" Aiu, my best friend, wrote 'bout   surfing at the North Shore with the tsunami waves breaking the bones.

Pedro "Boo" Arucan wrote 'bout   his rose-tattooed chest.

Domingo Bocalbos wrote 'bout   the uninvited bees who wrecked his birthday picnic, grinding all the *lumpias*, *pansit*, and pig's blood.

Jennifer Stewart wrote 'bout   the military importance of Hawaii.

Mary Ann Fujimoto wrote 'bout   spending Xmas at Hale Kipa cuz her mother lost it after her "other half" croaked from crystal meth.

Tyrone "Foots" White wrote 'bout   being popolo in Kalihi.

Joey "Boogaloo" Silva wrote 'bout   winning the 1st Annual Breakdancing Competition held at the State Capitol.

Mataele Mataele wrote 'bout   this road in the deep end of the valley diverging and he could not figure out which one to take, so he took the path that was less familiar, that had lesser footprints, and he ended up in Kahuku.

Purificacion "Twinkles" Batongbacal wrote 'bout   her sixth time.

V.

I wrote 'bout   :

Hungry bees eating space, black dogs losing it first time

America raiding Scotch-taped Kalihi while Pedros drowned in
    Franco's German-spit second time

Dim in the Philippines, G.I. Joes missing in Fort De Russy's
    dead-end pockets third time

Immigrants coming to Kalihi twinkling with their American
    crystal meth dream fourth time

Smiles that can break evil bones after school, culture
    breakdancing brawl in front of Gem's fifth time

Uninvited priests with their rose tattoos, grinding fighting cocks
    and preaching last words on a hundred-dollar altar sixth time

(And I wrote 'bout   a pig cap pen bleeding a hundred-dollar
    poem.)

Auntie Mary

Auntie of the 50th Star,
                 stop the insanity!
                           out your nephews and nieces now!
if you no more, go next door
                     out Lily's boy
can only shoot free throws when the moon's out
                            what kind NBA future that?
then out the McAllister band geek twins Pam and Lucy
after Pam and Lucy Ewing from Friday night's *Dallas*
                         (talk about tragic haoles
Black Tuesday dumped them in the Pacific Rim)
                             but look them now
now they cannot live without rice
now they substitute SPAM for ham
                       now they understand race
Pam's timpani rolls go with her bangs—uneven
Lucy, more butchy, get double-tongue clarinet solo in
     Selections from My Fair Lady
             you their Auntie too you know
you know you don't gotta be related by blood
                           to be related in Hawaii Nei
no forget everybody calabash cousins in the Austranesian chain
                           so take 'em to the movies
no tell 'em why that's between you and the matinee
when sneak previews come
                 sneak out or use Cecilia as excuse
tell 'em blackout bingo at the Officers Club, Hickam Air Force Base
                           they not going mind
just no be stingy with the cash
snack bars charge extra for butter nowadays
                 besides outing expensive not cheap
throw in bonbons, cab fares too
           you never know Auntie
you might chain-smoke your way to Vegas
you might find yourself double-parked in front the marquee
                           sooner than a blink
killing minutes with a nail filer

                        imagining their imagination getting used to the dark
blooming like flowers in a room of ice
                                        no doubt they thinking about you
wondering
how you know, Auntie?
                        how you know?
what you gonna tell 'em?
                        all new movies are old movies?
double-features are air-conditioned reruns?
                                        but say the hands lose tenderness
say the legs voluntarily part too late
                                or the heart runs out of fear
or the brain loses its rush
                        and then what?
Oh, Auntie, they goin' hate you with a 24-K
scramble you death threats for breakfast
                                steal your inch-thick Hawaiian bracelets
they goin' pawn 'em at Peter Pawn
                                they goin' blame their future on you
made-for-TV molesters they goin' be
                                over-achieving bowlers
suicide-by-water lyricists
                        or it could all end like this:
popsicle pathos for aliens with El Greco middle fingers
or Red-Vines-flavored yawns
                                but how they goin' beg Auntie
beg you for the next matinee
                        when, Auntie, when?

Sensory For Nine

I.

Freshman Banquet, 1983, John and I,
like the rest of the boys, went stag
but not to the hotel clerk who handed
us the keys to the Presidential Suite.
Once inside, we started a cheap dialogue,
scripted for ninth-grade porno boys
stranded on an improvised island
made of hard-ons and mermaids.
A bottle of half-filled whiskey
smuggled in for excuses and emptied
within minutes strategically stood
between us to perform a ritual: Skin,
which required a complete revolution
before the offering of tongues to men
who have perished in that unnamable
chasm some mistakenly call "passion."
The next day, he scribbled a short note
justifying the end of a friendship. It
was signed, Always.

II.

I met David, a Texan tourist, at the municipal
parking lot between Hamburger Mary's and God.
"On business?" I asked, "or pleasure?" He said
it didn't matter because he reasoned (with
a twang, of course) he was here to try
something new: Asian boys. He said he
got bored of tonguing sidewinder breaths and
doing honky-tonks who smelled in Marlboro
suits. He took me to his room and rammed his
ten-inch Southwestern cock up my ass without
a lubricant. Afterwards, he said it was the
best fuck he'd had in ages. "The fuck?"
I asked, "or me?" "Does it matter?" he asked.

I said it didn't. He flew back that night.
I squatted home, sore as hell. David was 47.
I was 15. It was my first time.

III.

I used to cruise Kuhio Avenue with a gold
crucifix around my neck because I'm Filipino,
Catholic, and superstitious. With the cross,
signed and blessed, I could ward off the
evil eyes of fag bashers and laser testicled
cops who patrolled my second home in golf
carts. One Sunday night, I hooked up with a
seminarian who wanted to test his temptation
and see if we spoke the same prayer of jism
to Jesus in a piss-stained alley near Saint
Augustine Church. "Just this once," he said,
and called me "my son." "Yes, Father." I
worked him hard in my mouth, the taste of
pre-confessional cum on the tip of my tongue.
He pulled my hair and guided me gently
until he shot Holy Trinity on my face and
the gold crucifix that gleamed in the dark.

IV.

Tom, a 70 year-old veteran, picked me up
in his BMW convertible at Ala Moana beach
park. He thought I had a million tricks
up my sleeves and offered me cash instead
of cookies. On the way to his condo,
he buried his hand in my crotch and said
it reminded him of World War II: my dick,
the US flag planted on Iwo Jima. Once
we got into the elevator, he pressed the STOP
button, crouched before me, pulled down
my zipper, and sucked me red, white, and
blue. I leaned against the carpeted wall,
pumped his mouth, and slapped him with stars
and stripes. Before leaving, I told him
I was Filipino, not Japanese, that he must

have meant Bataan and not Nagasaki or
Hiroshima. He apologized, said, "You all
look the same." I said, "And so do you."

V.

He threatened to arrest me, beat me with
his baton if I resisted, blow the whistle
to my parents, then leave me in a cell
to rot if I didn't bend over and spread
wide for his authorization. I obliged,
told him he could use his spit to fuck
me because all the cops I had were all
the same: all muscles, no meat. He jabbed
his three-inch badge inside me, moaned
things I had heard before—"You like my big
hard cock in your ass...oh yeah...such
a sweet little ass...oh yeah, oh yeah..."
I forgot his fuck, but remembered the
cologne he wore, the mole on his right thigh,
the yellow thread of his
shirt. Ten hours later, I dialed
the phone, spelled out his name to
a woman (his wife?) and told her about the
Drakkar cologne and the huge mole
next to the little mole that wanted
to eat me alive, yet couldn't.

VI.

Bert, a handsome teenager from New York,
met me when I was high on Ectasy and
down on Absolut shots. We cabbed four blocks
to his hotel where we swallowed more tablets
and downed more vodka in a room fit
for Persephone. We talked about traveling,
the natural high of taking off or swimming
through tunnels without a map or compass.
I leaned against the headboard and watched
the walls devour his shadow as he took off
his clothes. He said he hadn't been with a guy

before but had always had the urge to have
a man's flesh buried inside him. I believed
him, did him in, made him flinch as I had
flinched. He bit his lip as I dug
deeper than I had ever gone before. I
looked at his eyes, lost as the street light
that filtered through the cracks of the room.
I stared at his mouth, hungry as the walls
around us, and I stopped.

VII.

When I found out Bob, an Australian, had
a dick so fat it was made for Diamond Head
crater, it was already too late. He said
he wasn't into anal or oral, had a lover
back in Perth, and only needed a local fag
to chaperone him. After a Thai dinner,
Courvoisier, and a Jeff Stryker video, I passed
out on the floor whereupon he pounced on me
like a puma in heat. My rectum ripped
while the chandeliers of Hyatt rang
in my ears. Then he turned me around and
shoved his cock, thick as a baby's fist,
down my throat. I nearly gagged. It was
the first—and only—time I tasted cum
and blood.

VIII.

Gary, a haole visual artist who got rich and
famous sketching native boys, wanted to fist
me for two grand and a round-trip ticket to
Europe. I agreed only if we did it in his
yacht while I fucked Dario, his Filipino
boytoy. He said I was asking a lot; I said
that was what fisting was for. Sail away,
Dario said, and I blew him with one hand while
I jerked off with the other. Gary watched us
with a voyeuristic contempt as he poured baby
oil on his hands. I took my time, humped Dario

like a puppy, massaged his back, licked the sweat
off his neck, bit his earlobes. Before either
of us could come, Gary pulled me away, called me
a chinky fag and told me to scram. I left
without Penny Lane in my pockets, but I had
Dario's piece of ass still fresh on my cock.

IX.

I've had and been had by enough guys
to make a quilt and keep myself warm
forever, but I go on, open past wounds
to the night, stand or kneel or spread
in the dark, lick their sweat and five
o'clock shadows. I ask for more, ask for
the smell of salt on skin, the taste
of salt in my mouth, ask for the raw flesh
wanting more, giving more, but always,
never enough. Sometimes, when I'm alone
I jerk off to their names and shoot at the
what ifs, at the possibility of a fuck or
a blow-job session lasting longer than
a moan or the face of the clock; at
the moment when a stare at the crotch, an
opened fly, or an inviting grin means
breakfast in bed or flowers in a porcelain
vase; at the moment when an embrace or
a tongue means the making or breaking
of a night forgotten.

Valentine's Day

I am a single, thirty-something, detoxing
from too much British literature and
Asian American contemporary fiction.
Tonight's itinerary includes a Valentine's
nightcap with a fifteen-year-old Mondavi
and memories of losers and lovers,
like Pablo, who, on our first month anniversary
tossed me a copy of Jose Rizal's *Noli Me
Tangere* (Trans: Touch me not!), which
the Spaniards used to persecute the Chinese
Filipino mestizo novelist in 1895.
"Don't read too much between the lines,"
Pablo said, "I only bought it for under a buck
at the annual Friends of Library Book Sale,
President William McKinley High."

We broke up shortly thereafter.
Our separation caused by irreconcilable
differences on word preference: Revolution
vs. Insurrection, Modernity vs. Madernity.
With Pablo, love got lazy.
Endearments melted into imperatives,
sugar metabolized into remorse.
Pablo is now a hundred kisses old, like
Byong, exchange student from Seoul,
who served as both translator to
the Summer Olympics and beginner's
guide to "Short-Term Relationship in English
as a Second Language." Our mornings
were divided between kim chee-hot sex and
Greg Louganis displaying the mastery of gravity,
how the body could fall gracefully into blue.

That was 1988, when fornicating accompanied
translations and a tiger made of helium
floated to another world. After Byong,
I returned to my usual corner on the second

floor of Hamilton Library, right next to Folios
and Men's Room. There, I perused the canons,
reveling at my discovery that literature is nothing
more than a Camelot of words built especially
for those in search of the unexpected.

I completed my undergraduate creative thesis,
an apologia broken up into lines, dedicated
to lovers and strangers I had kissed
when nights were safe and sex wasn't prophylactic:
Pablo, Ramon, Dindo, Johann, Juan, Lucas,
Byong, Matt, Miguel, Ken, Kenzo, Kenji,

Mark, GWM, who drove a convertible BMW,
Platinum AMEX member since 1984,
marketing analyst for AT&T, long-distance
and supposedly monogamous lover
of four Ethnic-Studies-101 years to GAM,
chauffeured daily by the yellow Honolulu City
& County bus, green AMEX revoked in 1990,
former Comp Lit major, part-time public school
substitute teacher, part-Other, part-personal ad.

Four years we red-eyed it back and forth
between fog and dead volcanoes, took turns
cooking rice, bottoming, reading Rilke
passages, orgasming to Cole Porter's *Every Time
We Say Goodbye*, wondering which would
last longer: desire or our United Airlines mileage
plus account. Shit, why do they always come
at once, bother my buzz, make me want
to remember them all just so I can forget.

A Letter to Urbana in America from Her Seventy-Year-Old Sister Felisa

My dearest sister: Last night I learned
how to read the numbers in my blood.
They are like a compass. Too much
or too little of either north or south
means lie down and turn to CNN. Urbana,

we're still the only ones with cable TV.
It is no privilege at all since
the entire barrio walks in and out
as it pleases. I was thinking
of charging an entrance fee, passing out
a donation box, substituting an ice-
cold beverage stand for an air

conditioner. But we are all asthmatic
here: Not a single lung in this house
is immune to dust and heat. Anyway,
in case you missed it, President Estrada
was on CNN last night, discussing
the never-ending wars with Muslims
in the South, the communist army

up North, and the two types of women
in his life. Bill Clinton he said
has Hillary and Monica, while he
has Luisa and a multitude of X-chromosomes
who want nothing more in life

than to be impregnated by him. He said
this—can you believe?—on satellite
live before the camera replaced him
with a wounded nation crossing borders,
seeking refuge anywhere but home.

Is this our fate, Urbana? You there,
me here, wars and water between us? Oh,

I almost forgot, the good news: Tito
finally severed his ties with that

hija de muchacha, Julita, who took all
the time and liberty in the world to spread
to the congregation that her womb had opened
up, this announcement made prior to Doña
Corazon reading from the Gospel According
to Mark 4:3—Jesus and the four types
of soil, remember? Don't worry, I am doing
my best to drive that Hagar out of this town.

Thank God, I am walking again. Tito and
the children gave me an aluminum companion
for my seventieth birthday, so I am prepared,
step by step, in case you change your mind,
if only for a visit. Sincerely Yours, Felisa.

Requiem

Memory is a mosaic of tongues licking dirt, of lies embroidered to protect the King of Martial Law.

He was born. He is risen. He will kill again. And his kingdom will have no end.

Memory is a 1972 machine gun fired on Sunday morning. Four bodies on the edge of a dirt road. An act of suspended drowning.

This is a cup of his blood, the new and everlasting covenant.

Memory is a woman who howls wolf past curfew. Late night dinner parties and spilled champagne.

She drinks it so that their sins may be forgiven.

Memory is a spinning bottle, a top with no base, a mad pack of white dogs eating brown tails, brown dogs eating spotted tails.

She breaks the bread, gives it to their disciples, and says, Eat this in memory of us.

Memory is an archipelago of closed coffins, eaten calmly like sugared fingers of bread.

What Some Are Saying About the Body

"There are no dictators who can't be overthrown. There are only ones overthrown too late." Yevgeny Yevtushenko

Some say the body in a glass display case
in Batac, Ilocos Norte does not belong to you.

Nothing but wax in a freezer, some say;
on loan from Madame Tussaud's collection.

True or not, some say you shall remain on exhibit,
your death running on electricity,

until senators and widows can agree
to grant you a National Hero's burial in Manila

where, free from limbo alas,
you will join the company of veterans and American teachers.

There are some, however, who say you never left Hawaii,
that you are buried in Aloha soil,

along with piles of unpaid ICU and florist bills.
Some say you never owed a soul a single cent,

paid all your dues on time,
while others say you ran the country

like Mad Max with a credit card: No limit.
Some say you built the city from the swamp up,

that in one day plants rose into skyscrapers,
dust tracks became overpasses and,

for the first time, people walked across the sky,
like street angels in rubber slippers.

This is how you earned the title David Copperfield
of Urban Planning of Southeast Asia,

though some prefer to dub you George of the Jungle,
Lord of Dengue Mosquitoes,

Chief Editor of the *Encyclopedia of Missing Persons*,
unabridged edition.

Some say you were a magician indeed:
a grand illusionist who made hundreds of thousands

forget their identities
before you could exhale "Abracadabra!"

Some say Charles Bronson was your all-time favorite actor;
Death Wish your all-time favorite film.

A hundred percent fabrication is what some say
since you never owned a gun, drank bourbon,

chased platinum blondes.
It is brunettes, some say, brunettes in stilettos

that pumped your muscles and lengthened your penis
even till the last gasp;

death found you
under Honolulu sheets with a four-inch farewell.

Some disagree, argue you lost your libido
soon after you slipped inside a barrio bailarina.

Some say that your longest partner in bed was,
in fact, a dialysis machine.

Baloney, some say.
You never went limp, turned gray or yellow,

and lupus—what the hell is lupus, anyway,
but a foreign word to your body's vocabulary?

You died with the physique of a triathlete,
the original Thrilla from Manila, simple as that;

there are photographs and a museum to prove it.
But they're fake! some say, fake as

your World War II medals and Junior Featherweight belts.
All manufactured in Thailand, they say, where

your youngest daughter bought mutant orchids
and gold by the yard.

A line or two about the museum:
It contains only a stuffed monkey-eating eagle

and two dozen mannequins wearing your smile
that some say was manipulated,

like that of your eldest daughter who, some say,
had undergone more plastic makeover than Rubbermaid.

You had the memory of an elephant, some brag,
and in a day, had memorized Machiavelli's *The Prince*,

plus all the plum roles in Shakespeare's *Macbeth*.
A back-to-back one-man show

with a cameo by the First Lady as Lady Macbeth
in a negligee by Frederick's of Hollywood,

a pair of Charles Jourdan red pumps,
size eight, and a Rolex watch.

Wait a second,
they stashed all the country's money

in the Alps and we're giving them credit?
They're Bonnie and Clyde with amnesia, some say.

Off the South China Sea you converted an island
into a zoo, imported the best hunters, gatherers,

and scavengers from safari and Amazon.
Some say it was to show the world

that Man is capable of moving jungles,
while others say it was a birthday gift

to your one and only son who, some say,
received his Oxford diploma with an American Express receipt.

Some say you gave Michael Jackson how-to tips
on creating his own Mutual of Omaha Wild Kingdom.

Some say you were Robinson Crusoe and Noah in one.
And when the sloths, giant anteaters, coati mundis, and

gazelles disappeared into the jaws of jaguars,
hyenas, and anacondas, some say

they were replaced by writers, farmers, and students
held captive underneath Camp Crame.

What prisoners?
There were no prisoners, some say,

as there was no zoo,
oh, no,

none at all.
That island was, and still is, a beach resort

owned and run by a German hotelier from Düsseldorf
and his Filipina wife, a lounge singer.

Some say the Muzak played in your air-conditioned vault
is a requiem by Bach; others, Beethoven.

I saw his fingers move, some say,
to accompany organ chords or the Westinghouse hum.

Others say it is you beckoning the world to come,
come and feel the cold beating of your heart.

Exodus

(for N.V.M. Gonzalez)

I lit my computer screen and was about to email
America: Yes, I've had it with the bilingual
Maids next door doing laundry at four in the morning.
"What do you want me to do? They can't go to the
Fish market naked." This from my landlord.
I nearly went ballistic, but surrendered instead.
Whatever happened to courtesy, noise control,
Tenants' rights, lease on life? Before I could
Tell my mother to expect me in a week,
Two at the most, to fix the lock on
The door and make a spare, and to move
William back to the couch—I found a
hundred letters jamming my 14-inch mailbox. All by people
I didn't know or couldn't place, sadly informing me of
the passing of Philippine National Artist N.V.M. Gonzalez.

Little did my electronic informants know I was just
Around the corner—only traffic separated me from
The man of letters—getting ready to bite into a slice
Of a belated birthday cake when a professor and friend
Of the writer entered the teachers' lounge to say, "N.V.M.
Collapsed while undergoing dialysis, and is now brain dead."
Silence and sobs choked the room before the news
Drifted into the adjoining department, for grief no
Matter how controlled, can pass through even the
Thickest walls. Immediately I lost my appetite
For the sweetest things in life; it was replaced
By a recollection of my first encounter with
The writer whose main contribution to literature
Is his narratives about exiles in their own country.

Flashback: A crowded room about to be covered with
Kundiman music. The celebrated writer, for he
Had just been named National Artist, was in his cap
And had his cane. A poet, Abad, I think, introduced me to him.

"I commend you," he said, tapping his cane, "for using disco
Lyrics as a metaphor for the immigrant's All-American dream."
He then asked if I, too, practiced the aesthetics of simultaneity.
Or what he later explained as the ability to write and occupy
Two disparate spaces at the same time. "I don't know,"
I said, "but if you mean crossing a Manila street in front
Of moving vehicles with a poem in my head then the answer
Is yes." A friendship was formed in the here
And there. Unexpectedly, a thought invaded my head

Pushing a smile across my mouth. Don't you get it? I wanted
To shout to the faculty members. The man was gifted with
Words and symbolism: He was cleansing his blood
Before making his exodus, that cheeky guy. But I muzzled
The epiphany and went straight to Utopia Cybercafé.
Inside the chat room, I told my friend Lori in Seattle all about
The tragedy in Manila, the absurd thoughts that interrupted
My lament, how the word "dialysis" for some reason kept

Going in circles in my head. "A stubborn entry is always
Worth looking up," Lori, an etymologist, typed. "What
Are you hinting at?" I asked. "Break the word apart then
Go back to Greece," she said. Later that night, I looked up
"Dialysis" in the *Oxford Reference Dictionary*. What I found
Was a noun describing a ritual, i.e., purification via separation.
Then, sure enough, there it was: *dia*, meaning "through" or
"Across" and *lysis*, a suffix from *luo*, which is "to set free,"
And taking etymology into consideration, I, as an exile,
Comrade of Gonzalez, and student of words, dutifully obeyed.

Itinerary

7:56 a.m., Friday, February 21st. He finds his place in 20G, aisle seat. The stewardess goes on the PA system and thanks everyone for flying Philippine Airlines Flight 100. She also apologizes for the fourteen-hour delay. No one is complaining.

Not a single passenger is bitching because at 6:55 last night, which was Thursday, February 20th, all were chauffeured from the airport to the nearest five-star hotel. All, including Woody Harrelson, the bartender from the '80s TV sitcom *Cheers*.

At 7:25 p.m., Thursday, he surrendered his U.S. passport to the hotel desk clerk who mispronounced his name three times. Finally, he corrected her. The clerk, embarrassed, smiled, handed back the blue book with a thank you, then asked ("If I may, Sir") why he carried a German first and last name. Famished, he filled his plate at 8:05 p.m. with Japanese, American, and Filipino dishes from the all-you-can-eat buffet supervised by a chef from Singapore. He parked his ass next to Woody, who was sharing a table with a couple and their newborn. The mother, a blonde-haired Filipina, turned to him and asked, as he was preparing to shove a whole roll of *unagi* sushi into his mouth, if he didn't mind taking their pictures with the Hollywood celebrity who once fucked Courtney Love in *The People vs. Larry Flint*.

6:10 a.m., Friday, February 21st. He boards the shuttle bus and returns to the airport.

2:01 p.m. Aboard Flight 100, the map on the screen informs him that he is now crossing the International Date Line, which will separate the Philippines, the land of his birth, from Honolulu, where he has been living since 1977, by eighteen hours. The data that replaces the map reports that Honolulu is 1,490 miles and 90 minutes away. Tipsy from four glasses of cheap Merlot, he starts mumbling the numbers *à la* Willy Loman. 1,490 miles, 90 minutes away, 18-hour time difference…1,490 miles, 90 minutes away, 18-hour time difference…1,490 miles, 90 minutes away, 18-hour time difference….

The plane touches down on the tarmac of Honolulu International Airport. Born and raised in a household that thrives on Catholicism and Philippine folk superstition, he crosses himself three times and thanks St. Jerome (Anthony?) for a turbulence-free flight. The stewardess announces the time: 11:04 p.m. It is Thursday, February 20th.

10:20 a.m., Friday, February 21st. Forced to stop by a red light at King and Punchbowl intersection in downtown Honolulu. He is driving his mother's blue Taurus car, which smells of dogs and jasmine air freshener. Manila, his home for the last two months, re-enters his mind. He coughs until his lungs release a gray-speckled sputum. Detox begins.

11:55 a.m. His blood results show that he hasn't given up fast food. Dr. Lawler is putting him on Lipitor to lower his cholesterol level. "You only have one life to live, so live it fat-free."

12:18 p.m. In the parking lot of the medical building, he is suddenly seized by the urge to sing at the top of his lungs a Rodgers & Hammerstein tune.

12:39 p.m. The desert island choice narrows down to "Love, Look Away" from *Flower Drum Song* and "Bali Ha'i" from *South Pacific*.

12:41 p.m. He opts for "Chop Suey" (*Flower Drum Song*).

1:32 p.m. Korean mini-lunch plate at Yummy's on Dillingham Boulevard. Short ribs, kim chee, macaroni salad, and extra scoop rice.

3:55 p.m. He wakes up from a claustrophobic dream. In it, he is a nobody surrounded by loud Americans busily looking for themselves in wall-sized photographs by Andreas Gursky: an apartment building in Montparnasse; a Madonna concert; an underground station in São Paolo; a boxing match in Vegas. They leave the exhibit defeated, nauseous, pissed off at Gursky.

3:58 p.m. He composes a mental note: "In the eyes of Gursky, we are all a bunch of Find-Waldo's."

4:40 p.m. Sweat soaks his shirt as he climbs to the peak of the StairMaster.

5:31 p.m. Bikram Yoga in the sauna of his brother William's condominium.

6:45 p.m. Knife in hand, the man who makes his living washing cars in a Bret Easton Ellis novel stabs a kid in the stomach, in the throat, through his chin. The kid tries to fight back, but he's tied to a chair with a balled-up sock in his mouth. He dies looking at his killer's eyes, the color of sunset.

7:08 p.m. William calls to remind him of the 8 o'clock dinner with their friend Lisa at Mekong on Beretania, right across from Times and Grace's Drive-In.

7:49 p.m. He crosses the street to buy two bottles of Shiraz.

8:35:05 p.m. "Grant or no grant, I'm going back to Manila in June," he tells William and Lisa.

8:35:43 p.m. "What about the killer pneumonia?" Lisa asks.

8:35:59 p.m. "Or Bush's war in Iraq?" William says.

11:50 p.m. Lines of a could-be poem to accompany the jet lag. "Manila fucks you like a lover. Breaks your heart like a lover. Manila sings in the background of your sleep."

1:03 a.m. Saturday, February 22nd. Unable to sleep, he browses through an old issue of *Vanity Fair*, reads about a soiree that the Dalai Lama attended. Absent from the pictures, Richard Gere.

2:40 a.m. The mind is seeing doubles, thinking in two's. It dawns on him, finally, that he's just spent two Thursdays and Fridays in two cities.

4:12 a.m. He mixes an Ambien pill with Sprite, turns on the television, and prays that the VH-1 special, a rerun on the rise and fall of '70s teen heartthrob Andy Gibb, will give him the kind of sleep that the coke-addict teen heartthrob had before he went into cardiac arrest.

5:08 a.m. "Hula hoops and nuclear war," Rodgers & Hammerstein.

"Fluft drin Yalerick Dwuldum prastrad mirplush."
—Jonathan Swift, *Gulliver's Travels*
(Voyage to Laputa)

In Gulliver's translation:
"My Tongue is in the Mouth of my Friend."

Acknowledgments

Many thanks to the following journals and anthologies, in which some of the poems first appeared in slightly different versions:

Take-Out: Queer Writing from Asian Pacific America, Indiana Review, Hanging Loose, Philippine Sunday Inquirer Magazine, Philippine Free Press, Amerasia, POZ, Zyzzyva, Bamboo Ridge, Willow Springs, Returning a Borrowed Tongue, and *Premonitions: Kaya Anthology of North Asian American Poetry.*

Grants from National Endowment for the Arts and San Francisco Arts Commission, a one-year J. William Fulbright fellowship to the Philippines, and repeated visits to the MacDowell Colony made the writing of these poems possible. I am also grateful to the Virginia Center for the Creative Arts, the Millay Colony, and the Corporation of Yaddo.

A big *mahalo nui loa* to the following people who encouraged me, guided me, took care of me, and taught me that home is always in the plural form:

In the United States: Hyon Chu Yi-Toguchi, Paul Toguchi, David Azama, & Leif Meneke, who have been there pre-and-post Rolling; Jeffrey M. Rebudal & Allan P. Isaac, my lifeline on the East Coast; Ira Silverberg for encouraging me to write on; Karen-Tei Yamashita and Jessica Hagedorn, good friends & brilliant writers whose kick-ass writings continue to amaze and inspire me; Lucy Burns, Robyn Rodrigues, Wilma Consul, Marianne Villanueva, M. Evelina Galang, Noel Madlansacay, Pam Wu & the gang at the Asian Pacific Cultural Center in San Francisco.

In Hawaii: April Abe, who corrects my Pidgin; Bill Maliglig, Natalie Aczon, Bob Madison, Loretta Ables, Cindy Dudley, Shelley Nishimura, the fabulous Sunday gang at Mister Gordon Wong's; Laura Bach Buzzell, who repairs me whenever I'm home; Ruth Mabanglo, my bridge to Philippine culture and history; Dr. Sharon Lawler & her wonderful staff; my brother-in-law Greg Boorsma and the Northwest Airlines Honolulu crew who get me to Manila, in style, with class.

In the Philippines: Oscar Campomanes, The Artery, Jaime 'Bong' Antonio, Philippine-American Education Foundation, Rene Guatlo, Danton Remoto, Paolo Manalo, Shirley Lua, Karina Bolasco, and Goody Directo, who witnessed the process with patience and understanding.

Last, but not least, *maraming maraming salamat* to:

Faye Kicknosway, Lori Takayesu, Justin Chin, & Lisa Asagi, my source then and now

Bob Hershon, for saying YES

My hawk-eyed editors Ron Schreiber and Dick Lourie: you guys are the bomb!

&

My family—who despite everything—believed.

***

The editors of Hanging Loose Press would like to note that editing *Prime Time Apparitions* was the last task that Ron Schreiber performed for the press before his death in 2004. We believe that his love for Zack Linmark's work is reflected in the final book.